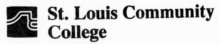

GIFTS
KIDS CAN
MAKE

SHEILA McGRAW

FIREFLY BOOKS

To Max and Graham

Edited by Sarah Swartz
Big photos by Joy von Tiedemann
Design, how-to photos and cartoons by Sheila McGraw
Typesetting, Parker Typesetting, London Ontario

Cataloguing in Publication Data

McGraw, Sheila
   Gifts kids can make

ISBN 1-895565-36-7 (bound) ISBN 1-895565-35-9 (pbk.)

1. Handicraft – Juvenile literature.
2. Gifts – Juvenile literature. I. Title.

TT160.M34 1994   j745.5   C94-931161-8

A FIREFLY BOOK

Published by:

Firefly Books Ltd.
250 Sparks Avenue
Willowdale, Ontario, Canada
M2H 2S4

Published in the U.S. by:

Firefly Books (U.S.) Inc.
P.O. Box 1325
Ellicott Station
Buffalo N.Y.
14205

Printed and bound in Canada

Contents

Getting Started

Appropriate gifts suit both the person and the occasion. And while a teddy bear for a baby, or socks for Father's Day are appropriate gifts, appropriate doesn't have to mean boring. There are loads of great gift ideas in this book that are imaginative and can be made to suit anyone!

OH GREAT, ANOTHER TIE.

Inappropriate gifts can sometimes be funny, like the new dad who buys his infant son a football, a baseball and all the gear even though the little kid is too young to sit up. Or imagine a Christmas where all the family's gifts get mixed up. *That* could be very funny, but it's still not very good. And of course live animals or gifts that are bad for someone's health are also inappropriate.

While all gifts are thoughtful, everyone knows that a handmade gift takes extra thought, time and care and that it is appreciated, remembered and kept longer. A handmade gift also makes for lots of conversation. Everyone will want to know how you made it, how long it took and where you got your ideas.

Age Groups

Sometimes a gift is good for any age group. For instance, a basket can be made with lots of different designs and colors and it can hold baby things or Grampa things.

When you make a gift for a baby or a toddler, make it safe, with no loose parts that can be swallowed or tangled around them.

Make something for older kids and grownups that suits their interests. They'll especially like a gift that is unique… and hand-made by you!

Money

Gifts don't have to be expensive. Almost all the gifts in this book are made from stuff usually found around the house.

Remember, not costing much doesn't mean the gift is worthless! Hand-crafted gifts are always considered the most valuable, because of the time and thought you've put into making them.

This Book

When you have looked through this book and decided on the gift you want to make, read through the whole project before you begin.

Next, collect all the materials and tools that you will need. This will eliminate the frustration of not having something when you need it.

With most instructions, you will see a column called "Read Me". Be sure to read this, before you start. It's full of helpful hints that will make your project go faster and easier.

Pages with patterns say "Wait! Don't cut this page!" This is to stop you from cutting up information on the back of the page and damaging your book. Instead of cutting the page, trace the pattern onto another sheet of paper.

When your gift is finished, see the section "Wrap It Up" for great wrapping and card ideas. There are also wrapping ideas throughout the book at the end of some projects. These are listed in the table of contents at the front of the book.

Terry Bunnies

Anyone would love to get a Terry Bunny. Give one all on its own, or include it as a special thoughtful addition in a basket of soaps or bath beads. It also makes a useful gift for a new baby.

These cute little bunnies are made from a facecloth. Some people will love the bunny just as it is and will keep it as an ornament for their bathroom or bedroom. Others will want to open up the bunny and use the facecloth. Just in case, use a craft glue that can be washed out for attaching the eyes and tail.

These Terry Bunnies are very easy to make and need no sewing. Simply fold a facecloth into the bunny shape and hold it all together with some ribbon. An extra pair of hands to help with holding and tying Bunny can come in handy.

Beginner's time to make Terry Bunny: less than half-an-hour.

How to do it

What You Need

Materials
- facecloth
- 18 in. (45 cm) string
- pompom for tail
- craft glue
- strong rubber band
- 24 in. (60 cm) narrow ribbon
- 2 small pompoms, or 2 googly eyes, or T-shirt paint for eyes

Tools
- scissors

Finished Size

◄— 4 in. (10 cm) —►

1 Remove any tags from the facecloth.
   Lay the facecloth flat. Beginning at one corner, tightly roll it to the center.

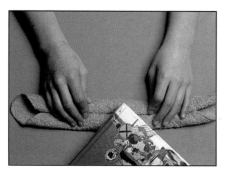

2 Place something heavy, like a book, onto the rolled-up facecloth, so that it won't unroll.
   Beginning at the opposite corner, tightly roll it to the center. You now have a long "double sausage" with pointy ends. The pointy ends will become Bunny's ears.

3 Fold the facecloth in half, so that the sausages are together and the smooth side is outside.
   Tie a piece of string around the center of the folded facecloth. Tie it in a bow, as you will need to remove it later.

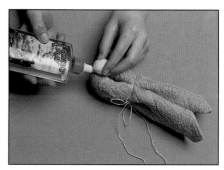

4 Glue the pompom tail to the facecloth, where it is bent.
   Allow the glue to dry.

5 Fold the facecloth again, at the string. The pointy ends should point toward the tail. Wind a strong rubber band around the facecloth to form Bunny's neck.

6 Untie and remove the string.

7 Tie the ribbon around Bunny's neck just behind the rubber band, making a bow on top. Remove the rubber band. Trim the ends of the ribbon, if you wish.

8 Make eyes. Glue small pompoms or googly eyes onto the Bunny's face. Or make two dots with T-shirt paint.

9 Take a bath with Bunny.

Make an attractive gift box for Bunny by gluing pictures to the outside of a large candy, coffee or popcorn can. Wash or wipe it out first! Then place some tissue paper, Bunny and his soaps inside and tie it all up with a ribbon.

Cotton Babies

Just one sock is what you need to make this cottony, huggable, washable baby toy. Kids and teens love Cotton Babies too, as a mascot for their locker or backpack.

Use a new sock for your Cotton Baby. Like real babies, all Cotton Babies are cute although they can look quite different from each other. It depends on the sock that you use. Some have long tops and some have short tops, some have lots of ribbing and some have no ribbing at all. And since socks come in pairs, make the left-over sock into a second Cotton Baby.

The Cotton Babies shown here have a matching ball on their hats that is made from the left-over piece of the sock. Finish your doll in the same way, or make a pompom (see "Birdies" page 16). Our Cotton Babies have little dots for eyes, made with T-shirt paint. You can also give yours a smiley mouth or blushing cheeks. It's up to you.

Beginner's time to make Cotton Baby: under one hour.

How to do it

What You Need

Materials
- paper and pencil
- ladies-size, cotton sock
- thread to match sock
- 3 handfuls of white, polyester stuffing
- 2 beads, buttons, T-shirt paint, or needle and thread, for eyes

Tools
- ruler or tape measure
- scissors
- a few pins
- sewing needle

Optional
- pompom for hat
- craft glue
- 10 in. (25 cm) ribbon

Finished Size

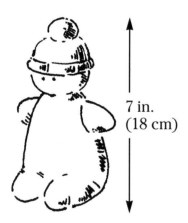

7 in. (18 cm)

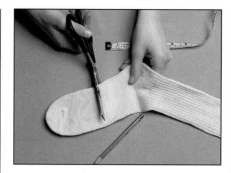

1 Trace the pattern pieces on page 14 onto paper. Cut out the patterns.
Lay the sock flat on its side. Measure and mark 4 in. (10 cm) from the heel toward the toe. Cut across the sock at the mark. Save the sock's toe and set it aside.

2 Turn the sock inside out. Flatten the front.

3 Pin the LEGS pattern onto the flat sock, with the curved ends of the legs at the cut edge of the sock. Cut along the cutting line.

4 Pin the legs. Sew by hand or machine, near the edge. (See *Sewing* in the "Read Me" section.)

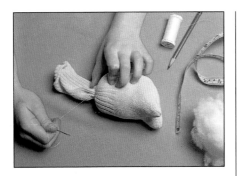

5 Turn the sock right-side-out.

To make the neck, measure and mark halfway from the heel to the top of the sock. Fill with stuffing up to the mark.

Sew stitches around the sock at the mark.

Pull the stitching tight to gather it. Tie off your sewing.

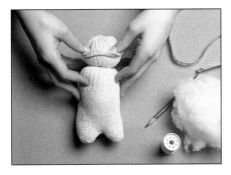

6 To make the head, measure and mark halfway from the neck to the top of the sock. Fill with stuffing to the mark. Sew around the sock at the mark and gather tightly.

Fold the ribbing down to create the hat. There will be a small hole at the centre of the hat. Don't worry. This will be covered later with a pompom.

7 Find the toe that you cut off the sock. Turn it inside out and flatten it. It will be two layers.

Pin the ARMS pattern to the two layers of toe and cut it out. Do it again.

8 Pin the arms and sew around the curved edges. Do not sew the straight sides closed.

9 Turn one arm section right-side-out. Fill it with stuffing. Turn the open sides in and sew them closed. Do it again.

Read Me

Marking
The markings that you make for Cotton Baby are only temporary. A pin or a stitch of thread can make a good marker, instead of a pencil or pen which may show.

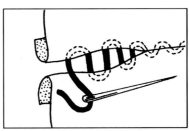

Sewing
When sewing two flat pieces together, such as the legs or arms, use tiny stitches. You may want to sew the seam twice to make it tight and strong. To sew the arms to the body, use a ladder-stitch, shown above, which is almost invisible.

Tying Off
When you have finished sewing, make a tight knot, so the stitches won't undo. Do this by making a loop under your last stitch and drawing the needle through it. Repeat.

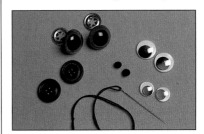

Eyes
If you are making this doll for a baby, don't use sewn-on beads or buttons, or anything else that may come off easily. They could be swallowed by the baby. Instead, use T-shirt paint or sew dots for eyes.

10 Pin one arm to each side of the body. The straight edge of the arm should be against the body.

Sew the arms in place. (See *Sewing* in the "Read Me" section.)

11 Make eyes either with two dots of T-shirt paint, or by sewing dots with colored thread. (See *Eyes* in the "Read Me" section.)

12 *Optional:* Instead of using a pompom, make a round ball for the top of the baby's hat. Using the leftover toe of the sock, cut a circle about 2 in. (5 cm) across. Sew and gather around the edge. Stuff the ball, as you pull the gathers tight. Tie off.

13 Glue or stitch the pompom or the ball to the top-centre of the hat. Allow it to dry. Tie a ribbon around the baby's neck, if you wish.

WAIT! DON'T CUT THIS PAGE!

If you cut out these patterns, you will destroy important information on the back of this page. Instead of cutting, trace the pattern onto a sheet of paper.

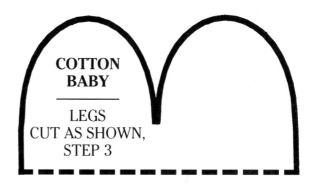

COTTON BABY

LEGS
CUT AS SHOWN,
STEP 3

COTTON BABY

ARMS
CUT 4

*Even a lunchbag can look like deluxe wrapping.
Cotton Baby fits perfectly into this lunchbag
which has been splatter painted. The tissue
paper and ribbon add a festive touch.*

Birdies

Perch Birdie in a baby's crib, on a window-sill or on a bookshelf. Anywhere he nests, he looks cuddly and chirpy. You can make your little bird in any color combination you like: bright tropicals, pale pastels or speckled grays. It's up to you.

This bird is made from two pompoms, one large for the body and one small for the head. These pompoms are made differently from the pompoms for Fuzzy Kitty (page 36). The Birdie pompoms take more time, but they are stronger. And since there are only two pompoms to make, it's not a big job.

This little bird makes a great stocking stuffer or baby shower gift.

Beginner's time to make Birdie: one to two hours.

How to do it

What You Need

Materials
- paper and pencil
- cereal box cardboard
- 2 balls of light to medium weight yarn
- dental floss or string
- scrap of felt, for beak
- craft glue
- length of black yarn, for eyes

Tools
- scissors
- ruler
- wool needle or darning needle

Optional
- crochet hook

Finished Size

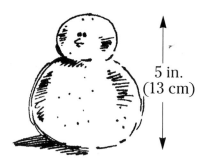

5 in. (13 cm)

1 Trace the pattern pieces on page 20 onto paper. Cut out the HEAD and BODY patterns. Trace around each twice onto cardboard. This will give you four cardboard "donuts".

Cut out the cardboard donuts. (See *Cutting Centers* in the "Read Me" section.) Mark the tummy and back colors. Snip small notches at each mark.

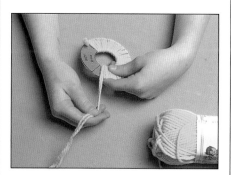

2 Make the body pompom. Start with the tummy color. (Our Birdie's tummy color is yellow.) Cut a double length of yarn. You may want to make your bird speckled. (See *Speckles* in the "Read Me" section.)

Place the two large cardboard donuts together. Tuck one end of the double yarn into a notch and wind the yarn around the donuts.

Make one row, filling between the marks. Don't cut the yarn. (See *Adding Yarn* in the "Read Me" section.)

3 Start your second color. This will be Birdie's back. (Our Birdie's back color is blue.) Make one layer. The donut is now covered in one layer of yarn. Don't cut the yarn.

4 Going back over the same colors, make a second layer. Continue making layers. As the hole becomes smaller, you may find a crochet hook helpful for pulling the yarn through the center hole.

5 Stop using the tummy color when the center hole is ¾ in. (2 cm) across. Continue *using only the back color.* This will make Birdie's wings.

Thread a needle with the yarn when the hole becomes very small. (See *Threading Needle* in the "Read Me" section.) When no more yarn goes through the hole, you know you are finished.

6 There are two ways to cut the pompom.

To make a pompom that is round like a ball, cut around the edge, next to the donut.

Or you can slide your scissors under the yarn, between the two cardboard donuts and cut the yarn. This method will make an oval pompom.

7 Using the dental floss or string, tie it around the center of the pompom between the two cardboard donuts. Pull the dental floss or string as tight as possible and tie well.

Starting at one of the notches, tear the cardboard and remove it. Fluff up the pompom and trim any long yarn or knots.

8 Make the pompom for the head. Repeat steps 2 through 7, using the HEAD pattern.

Read Me

Cutting Centers
To cut the center of your cardboard "donut", poke a hole in the cardboard with the tip of your scissors. Or fold the cardboard and cut into it. Then cut out the center.

Making Layers
On your first layers, you will be able to see between the yarn. To keep the layers as tight as possible, try pushing the yarn together with your fingers as you go along.

Adding Yarn
Add new lengths of yarn as you run out, by either tying the new piece to the last piece, or by laying the new piece onto the pattern and holding it in place with your finger to get started.

Threading Needle
To thread a needle with yarn, loop the yarn over the needle. Holding the yarn tight, draw it off the point. This will flatten the yarn. Press the flattened yarn through the eye of the needle. Or use a needle threader.

Speckles
You can make a speckled bird by winding another color in with the back or tummy color in an irregular way.

9 Trim any hanging strings and position the head on the body. Thread a needle with dental floss or string. Tie the head and body pompoms together, slipping the needle and thread through the center of each pompom. Pull and tie them together tightly.

10 Cut the beak out of felt. Fold the beak in half, so the points are together. Fold it in half again along its length.

Position the beak on the head by spreading apart the yarn. Glue the beak in place.

11 For eyes, thread the needle double, with a length of black yarn. Draw the needle through the head where you would like the eye. Pull the thread through until it is level with the cut ends of the yarn. Cut it short at the back of the head. Repeat for the second eye.

WAIT! DON'T CUT THIS PAGE!

If you cut out these patterns, you will destroy important information on the back of this page. Instead of cutting, trace the pattern onto a sheet of paper.

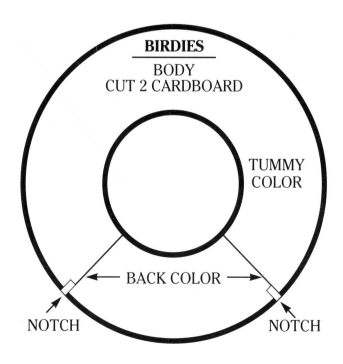

BIRDIES
BODY
CUT 2 CARDBOARD

TUMMY COLOR

← BACK COLOR →

NOTCH

NOTCH

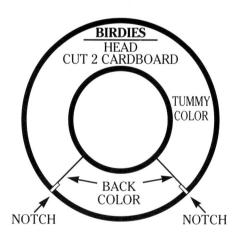

BIRDIES
HEAD
CUT 2 CARDBOARD

TUMMY COLOR

← BACK COLOR →

NOTCH

NOTCH

BIRDIES
BEAK
CUT 1 FELT

We made an egg for Birdie to sleep in until he gets hatched at the birthday party. He was wrapped first in bright tissue paper, then in aluminum foil. Foil is good for wrapping odd shapes because it stays in the shape you bend it. The ribbon and the "thought balloon", which was cut from light-weight cardboard, add extra fun.

Apple Cinnamon Ornaments

In the fall and winter, nothing smells more homey and inviting than the apple-cinnamon smell of pie or hot cider. Now you can give this aroma in a gift of great-looking ornaments. Change their shape and how they're presented to suit the occasion.

Not only is this project super-simple, it also doesn't require baking, unless you want to speed up the drying process. And because the ingredients are just apple sauce, flour and cinnamon, little kids can make these decorations safely. When you mix the ingredients, they will be a dark brown color. As they dry, the color will change to the color of natural clay. If you decide to bake them, you will fill your house with the smell of apple-cinnamon. Remember that the ornaments will not be completely dry when they come from the oven. But, once they have cooled, they can be handled, decorated, hung up or wrapped.

Use either a small knife, cookie cutters or the rim of a glass to cut shapes.

Beginner's time to make ornaments: twenty minutes preparation, two hours baking, or two days drying.

How to do it

What You Need

Ingredients
- ⅓ cup (75 mL) cinnamon (one standard jar)
- ⅓ cup (75 mL) flour
- ⅔ cup (150 mL) applesauce

Tools
- measuring cup
- mixing bowl
- fork
- mixing spoon
- cutting board
- rolling pin or jar
- knife or some cookie cutters
- straw or ballpoint pen
- cookie sheet or drying rack
- ribbon

Yield
Makes approximately twelve ornaments.

1 Preheat your oven to 225°F (100°C), if you wish to bake your ornaments. Measure the cinnamon and flour and put both into a bowl. Mix with a fork.

2 Measure and add the applesauce to the flour and cinnamon. Mix with a mixing spoon. You may think that it will never all mix together, but keep going. It will! The dough will be thick and stiff.

3 Place the dough onto the cutting board. (Note to all grown-ups: *Don't* flour the cutting board!) Using a rolling pin or the side of a jar, flatten the dough and roll it until it is ¼ in. (.5 cm) thick.

4 Cut out your ornaments with a cookie cutter or a small knife. (See *Cutting* in the "Read Me" section.)

5 Using a straw or a ball point pen, make a hole near the top, big enough to get the ribbon through.

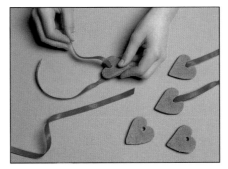

Cutting
Experiment with shapes. A wreath shape can be made by using a glass to cut the big circle and a cinnamon jar top to cut the small circle inside.

You can also make marks and designs on the top of the dough.

When you cut out the shapes, gather all left-over dough, roll it out again and cut out more shapes. Keep going until all of the dough is used up.

6 Place the shapes on a cookie sheet and place in the oven. Bake for two hours. Put on the timer, so that you don't forget them.

If you don't want to use the oven, place the shapes on a drying rack where they can dry without being in the way. If you don't have a rack, turn them over twice each day. Allow them two days to dry.

7 When the ornaments are dry, thread a piece of ribbon through the hole and tie the ends.

You can also string them in a row on lace, braid, cord, or the belt loops on the waistband from some old jeans. There are lots of great ways to display these wonderful smelling ornaments.

A shaped bag is ideal for a small gift. For instructions to make your own unique bag see "Shaped Bag", page 85. The instructions are for a Doggie bag but you can alter the shape and design of the bag to be anything you like.

Citrus Ornaments

Oranges, lemons and limes have long been used for pomanders, those nice smelling decorations that are studded with cloves and tied up with ribbon. The warm glowing colors, interesting textures and the patterns of their segments have made dried citrus fruit popular for making decorations. In this project, we'll show you how to make three different citrus decorations: pomanders, a wonderful smelling traditional gift for any occasion; dried-orange medallions for decorating a Christmas tree or adding to a dried arrangement; and topiaries, (pronounced toe-pee-air-ees) made from dried grapefruit, which glow like luminous sunflowers when placed on a window-sill with their backs to the sun.

All three projects are a great way to use up any citrus fruit that may be past its prime. They're simple to make and they give great results when you are finished. The medallions and the topiaries will require some low-temperature baking at first to partially dry the fruit and will then need several days or weeks to air dry. Remember, dried fruits, flowers and foliage always need air circulation. Never store them in a plastic bag.

How to do it

Pomanders

The pomander will dry slowly and become darker, harder and lighter in weight. It will also shrink. When it is new, it must hang freely, away from other objects. Otherwise it will mold. When completely dry, it can be added to a dried arrangement.

What You Need
- lemon (substitute a lime or orange, if desired)
- ribbon
- pins
- pen
- knitting needle
- cloves

1 Roll the fruit under the palm of your hand to soften it.

2 Wrap one long piece of ribbon around the fruit, crossing it at the bottom and bringing it up the sides. It should divide the fruit into quarters. Pin the ribbon in place as you go.

3 Draw along all sides of the ribbon with a pen. Remove the ribbon.

4 Beginning at the top of one of the quarters between the ribbon-lines, make a hole with the knitting needle. Insert the stem of a clove into the hole. Make another hole near it and insert another clove. Continue until the area is covered with cloves.

Repeat for the remaining three sections.

5 Replace the ribbon in the same way you attached it in step 2, pinning it where necessary. Tie it in a square knot at the top, close to the fruit. Don't trim the ribbon.

Tie the ends of the ribbon together, making a loop for hanging. If you wish, add other decorations at the knot closest to the fruit.

Medallions

These rustic looking discs are dried slices of orange. When they are dry, they are a warm brown-orange tone and look best when they are added to an arrangement of seed pods, pine cones or dried flowers. They also look wonderful as ornaments on a Christmas tree.

What You Need
- 3 oranges
- knife
- cutting board
- cookie sheet
- drying rack
- ribbon

1 Preheat your oven to 200°F (95°C).
On the cutting board, slice the oranges ¼ in. (.5 cm) thick. Make sure you cut across the fruit so that the segments show. (This is a juicy job.)
You can either pick out the seeds or leave them in. I like them left in.

2 Place the slices on a drying rack and place the drying rack onto a cookie sheet. Bake the slices for two hours. Set the timer so that you don't forget them.
When the slices come out of the oven, they will be leathery, still soft and a bit sticky.

3 Allow them to air-dry for about one week. Placing them on a radiator, heater or window-sill will help. When they are dry, place them in an arrangement.

4 To use as decorations for a tree, poke a hole through the slice near the rind and thread a ribbon through. Tie the ends of the ribbon together to make a loop for hanging.

Topiary

These instructions make one topiary (with some grapefruit slices left over). While one looks great on its own, you may want to make a grouping. A grouping looks best with an odd number of topiaries – three or five – and with the sticks at different lengths.

What You Need

- 1 grapefruit, pink or white inside
- knife
- cutting board
- drying rack
- cookie sheet
- small clay pot
- small block of florist's foam (known as oasis)
- narrow twig, about 8 in. (20 cm) long
- handful of moss (available at florist shops)

1 Preheat your oven to 200°F (95°C).
On the cutting board, cut the grapefruit into ¼ in. (.5 cm) thick slices. Cut across the fruit so that the segments show.

2 Place the slices on a drying rack and place the drying rack onto a cookie sheet.
Bake the grapefruit for two to three hours. Put on the timer so that you don't forget about it.

3 Remove the grapefruit from the oven. The slices will be soft and mushy. So don't move them or they will tear.
Make a small slit in the skin to insert the stick later. Allow the grapefruit to air-dry on the rack for one to two days. Check that it is fairly firm.

4 Prepare the base. Cut the oasis and place it in the pot. It should be a tight fit.

5 Insert one end of the stick into the slit of the grapefruit, pushing the stick to the center of the slice. This will be easier if the stick is cut to a point. Be sure the grapefruit is not stuck to the rack. Otherwise, when you lift it on the stick, it will tear.

Push the other end of the stick into the oasis in the pot.

6 Place the moss on top of the pot to hide the oasis. The grapefruit slice will continue to dry for two to three weeks.

7 Just add sunshine.

Not all gifts need to be completely covered by wrapping. Bouquets and other awkwardly shaped presents can be placed in an open box. Then gather wrapping or tissue paper around the box and tie it up with a ribbon.

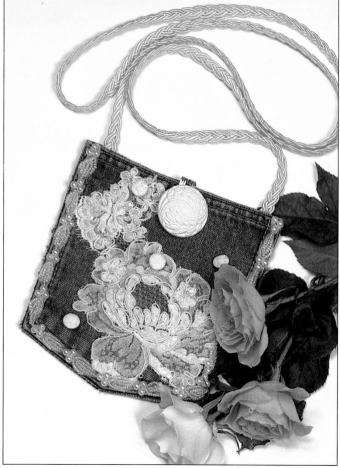

Pocket Purse

McGraw's law of blue jeans says that everyone has three pairs. One that you wear a lot, one that doesn't fit and one that is out of style. Ask very nicely and someone may let you have their discarded jeans. You'll need the two back pockets for the purse. And don't throw away the rest! Old jeans can be used for other projects.

This purse is very easy and lots of fun to make. It can be worn anywhere from school to parties to the movies to shopping. Its two pockets are big enough to carry the things you need.

The best way to decorate these purses is to rummage around the house. Old lace, sequins, beads, buttons, braid, iron-on decals and bits of old out-of-style costume jewelry can all be glued or stitched on, leaving a little or a lot of the denim showing. You'll have to *tell* people you made this, because they won't know by looking. They'll think it was bought in a boutique!

Beginner's time for Pocket Purse (not including rummaging or drying times): less than two hours.

How to do it

What You Need

Materials
- a pair of jeans with matching backpockets
- 1⅓ yd. (1.3 m) braid, or heavy ribbon for strap
- thread to match pockets
- button or other closure (can be the jeans' button)
- decorations
- strong craft glue or white carpenter's glue
- plastic grocery bag
- bunch of imagination

Tools
- scissors
- sewing needle
- a few pins

Finished Size

← 6 in. →
(15 cm)

1 Cut the back pockets out of the jeans. Cut close to the pockets, but be careful not to cut into them. Leave any labels attached. The two pockets should match, but put them together to check.

2 To make the loop for the closure, cut 8 in. (20 cm) off the end of your strap. Fold the closure in half and place it on the back of one pocket in the center, with the loop overhanging the top edge. Position your button on the pocket and test the length of the loop to close over the button. Put the button aside.

Stitch the loop in place. Be careful not to sew the pocket shut.

3 Lay the ends of your strap onto the back of the same pocket, just inside the pocket seams. If you are using a flat strap like ribbon, check that it is not twisted. Stitch the ends in place.

4 Decorate the front of one pocket. The other pocket will be the undecorated side of the purse that goes against the body when it is carried.

Lay your decorations and the button for the closure in place on the pocket. Pin them in place.

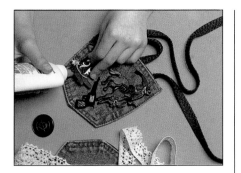

5 Glue, iron on, or stitch the decorations to the pocket, *except for the closure button.* If you use glue, place a piece of plastic, cut from a grocery bag, inside the pocket so that the glue that soaks through won't stick the pocket shut. Allow it to dry.

6 *Optional:* If you want to edge your purse with lace or fringe, lay one pocket wrong-side-up. Apply glue near the sides and bottom edges. Lay the lace or fringe on top of the glue.

7 Lay one pocket wrong side up. Apply glue near the edge along the sides and bottom. Also apply glue along the top, *but away from the edge.*

Place the wrong side of the other pocket onto the glue, matching the edges. Put plastic inside the tops of both pockets. Place a phone book on top and allow to dry.

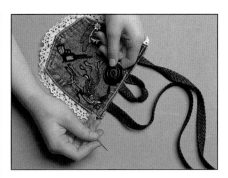

8 Put the button for the closure in place. Test it by closing it. Sew it in place.

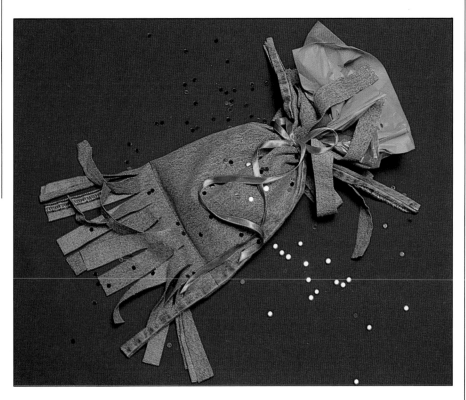

For a unique gift wrap, cut a piece of leg from the blue jeans. Sew across the leg about 6 in. (15 cm) from one end. Cut into the end to create fringe. Place your gift inside, tie up the open end and cut again for a streamer effect.

Fuzzy Kitty

Know a cat lover? Who doesn't! Fuzzy Kitty is an almost life-sized, floppy, loveable, low-maintenance cat. She needs no litter or fishy-smelling cat food. This is a great gift for cat lovers of all ages. Choose your yarn colors to match the cat lover's cat – marmalade orange, Holstein (white with black cow spots), solid colors, tabby stripes, or Oreo (black head and tail, white body).

Maybe you made pompoms when you were little and you may think pompoms are hokey and old fashioned. But when these pompoms are transformed into cats, they are amazing. And they're super-easy to make!

Beginner's time to make Fuzzy Kitty: three hours.

How to do it

What You Need

Materials
- paper and pencil
- cereal box cardboard
- 3 balls of chunky yarn
- string or dental floss
- 1 felt square for ears (felt to match yarn), for ear-backs
- 1 pink felt square, for ear-fronts and nose
- craft glue
- 2 craft eyes (available at craft stores)

Tools
- scissors
- ruler
- a few pins

Finished Size

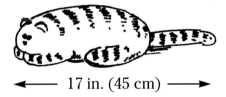

← 17 in. (45 cm) →

1 Trace all pattern pieces on pages 40 and 41 onto paper. Cut out the patterns and trace around them onto cardboard.

Cut out the cardboard pieces and their center holes (see *Cutting Centers* in the "Read Me" section), and snip the notches.

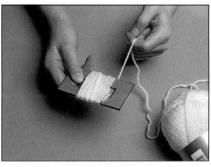

2 Make the legs. The first pompom will be the cat's foot. If you want your cat to have white feet, use white yarn.

Unroll some yarn, but don't cut it. Tuck the end of the yarn in the notch of the pattern. Wind the yarn around the pattern 12 times side by side, making a neat row. Don't cut the yarn.

Wind the yarn around the pattern another 12 times, going back to the start. Cut the yarn and tuck the end into the notch or under the yarn.

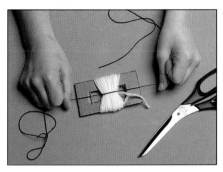

3 Cut a piece of string or dental floss the length of your arm. This will be called the "string".

Tuck the ends of the string through the holes on either side of the yarn. Center the string and tie a very tight knot, bunching the yarn. (See *Tying String* in the "Read Me" section.)

Do not trim the ends of the string.

4 Slide scissors under the yarn and cut the yarn along the two outside edges of the cardboard. Gently pull the cardboard off the pompom.

If you are making a striped cat, change colors for each pompom.

5 Repeat steps 2 and 3. Tightly tie this pompom with the ends of the string from the first pompom. Now you have two pompoms, joined together. Repeat step 4.

Make five more pompoms (seven altogether) tying them together with the string until you have a 6 in. (15 cm) sausage shape. Do not trim the ends of the string.

Make three more matching legs (four altogether). Don't trim the strings. Set the legs aside.

7 Make a body pompom. Wind the yarn around the BODY pattern twenty times on each layer, for four layers.

Use the string from the tail to tie the body pompom.

Attach two back legs. Tie the string on one leg in a knot 1 in. (2.5 cm) from the last pompom, creating a loop. Slip the loop over the string from the body pompom. Repeat with a second leg.

Cutting Centers
To cut the centers of your patterns, carefully use a knife or your scissors to poke a hole in the center, or fold the pattern and cut into the fold. Then slip your scissors through the hole and cut.

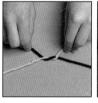

Tying String
The string that holds your pompom together must be tied very tightly. Otherwise the cat will fall apart. A regular knot, shown in photo on the left, may slide open, *try looping the string twice*, as shown on the right. Pull tightly. Then tie once or twice more.

6 Make the tail. Repeat steps 2 through 5 using the TAIL pattern. But this time wind the yarn only ten times back and forth, across the pattern. Make the tail about 8 in. (20 cm) long, (ten to twelve pompoms). Do not trim the ends of the string.

8 Make three more body pompoms, tying them on as you go, in front of the legs.

Add the remaining two legs as you did with the back legs (see step 7). Then make and add two more body pompoms. You should have six body pompoms altogether.

Adding String
As you tie the pompoms together, you may run out of string. When this happens, just tie on more string. Use a knot that won't slip.

9 Make the face pompom. Wind the yarn around the FACE pattern fifteen times for each layer, making three layers.

Tie the face to the body. Trim the ends of the string.

10 Pin the EARS and NOSE patterns to the felt and cut along the cutting line. Cut two pink ears, two matching ears and one pink nose.

Glue one pink ear-front to one matching-color ear-back. Repeat for the second ear. Allow them to dry.

Attach the ears by parting the yarn on the head of the cat and gluing the ears into the parted section, with the pink sides facing forward.

Glue the nose and eyes in place on the cat's face.

Examine your cat and trim any long "hairs".

WAIT! DON'T CUT THIS PAGE!

If you cut out these patterns, you will destroy important information on the back of this page. Instead of cutting, trace the pattern onto a sheet of paper.

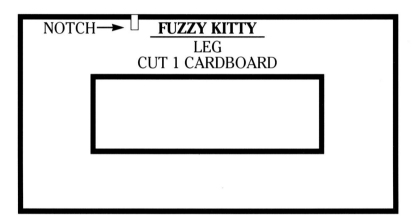

FUZZY KITTY
NOSE
CUT ONE FELT

FUZZY KITTY
EAR
CUT 4 (2 PINK)

NOTCH→ **FUZZY KITTY**
LEG
CUT 1 CARDBOARD

NOTCH→ **FUZZY KITTY**
FACE
CUT 1 CARDBOARD

NOTCH→ **FUZZY KITTY**
TAIL

CUT 1 CARDBOARD

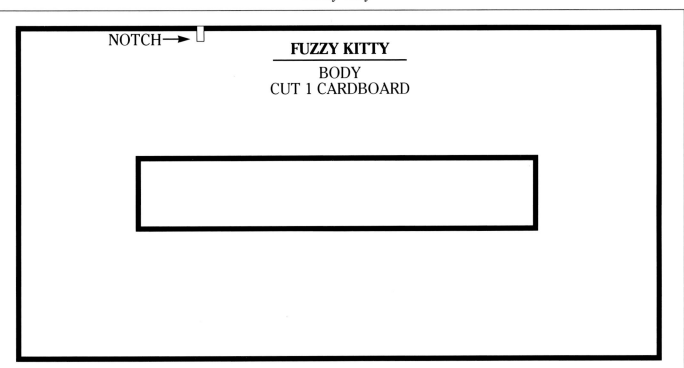

NOTCH →

FUZZY KITTY

BODY
CUT 1 CARDBOARD

*To create some excitement, wrap Fuzzy Kitty
(or any other soft toy) in a box that is covered
with brown Kraft paper or newspaper and tied
up with string. Punch some "air holes" and write
"wild beast inside" on the box.*

Kitty's "Doormouse"

Is this a gift for a cat or the cat's owner? Both! Kitty will love her big mouse because it's a scratching post. Kitty's human will appreciate it because the "Doormouse" will entice Puss away from shredding the sofa. Doormouse also looks great and hangs out of the way on a doorknob.

Choose a fairly sturdy fabric for this mouse. A heavy sweatshirt knit is good, especially since it won't fray. This makes it easier to work with. An upholstery type of fabric can also work well. You don't have to stick with mouse-gray as a color. Be as crazy as you like. Use buttons, beads or felt for the eyes, and Snowball, Jiggers and Clawdia would appreciate a jingle bell on the tail. To get a cat interested in "Doormouse" right away, sprinkle some catnip inside the mouse, before you close it up.

Beginner's time to make Kitty's "Doormouse": one to two hours.

How to do it

What You Need

Materials
- pen and paper
- corrugated cardboard
- 24 in. (60 cm) square of fabric for body
- 8 in. (20 cm) square of pink fabric for ears
- 1½ yd. (1.5 m) yarn or macrame rope
- strong craft or carpenter's glue
- needle and thread
- 2 eyes
- stuffing
- plastic bag
- masking tape

Tools
- scissors
- pins
- stapler

Optional
- jingle bell
- art knife
- catnip

Finished Size

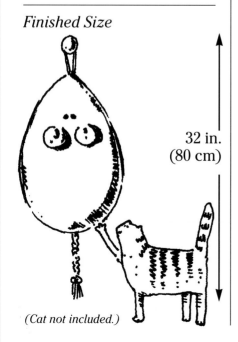

32 in. (80 cm)

(Cat not included.)

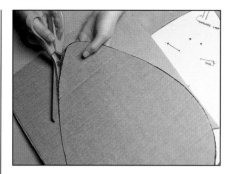

1 Use a photocopier or pen and paper to enlarge the patterns on page 47 to the correct size. (See *Drafting Patterns* in the "Read Me" section.) Cut out the enlarged patterns.

Trace around the BACK-TUMMY pattern onto cardboard. Cut it out. An art knife works best for this.

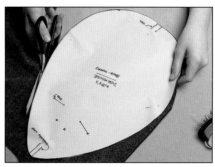

2 Pin the BACK-TUMMY pattern to one layer of the body fabric. Cut along the cutting line.
Do not cut any slashes for ears, tail or hanging loop in this piece. Put this TUMMY piece aside.

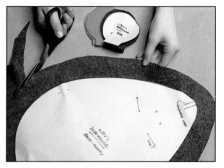

3 Pin the BACK-TUMMY pattern to one layer of the body fabric. Cut 3 in. (7.5 cm) *larger* than the pattern all around. This will be the BACK. Cut the slashes for the ears, rope and tail as shown on the pattern. Mark the eyes.

Pin the EAR pattern to two layers of body fabric. Cut them out. Repeat with two layers of pink fabric.

4 To make the tail, cut three lengths of yarn or macramé rope, each 12 in. (30 cm) long. Staple and glue the ends to the cardboard where it is shown on the pattern.

5 Braid the yarn. (See *Braiding* in the "Read Me" section.)

Tie a knot in the end or sew together. Attach a jingle bell, if you wish.

7 To make an ear, place two ear sections (1 pink and 1 body color) with their wrong sides together. Sew close to the edge with a sewing machine or by hand. Repeat for the other ear.

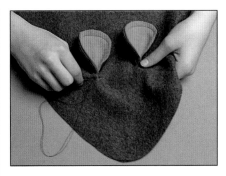

9 Lay the BACK piece of fabric flat, right side up, with the point at the top. Insert the ears into the slashes, as shown, with their pink sides up. Stitch the bottoms of the ears to the body.

6 To make the hanging loop, cut one length of yarn or rope 16 in. (40 cm) long. Fold it in half.

Staple and glue the ends to the top point of the cardboard, as shown on the pattern.

8 Lay one ear flat with the pink side up and the straight edge at the bottom. Fold the sides in to the center. Sew across the bottom edge. Do this again with the other ear.

10 Attach the eyes where they are marked on the pattern. Use any type of eyes you like: buttons, craft eyes, felt cut-outs or T-shirt paint.

Read Me

Drafting Patterns
To enlarge a pattern by hand, make a grid of 1 in. (2.5 cm) squares. Most cutting boards have a grid printed on them which can be seen through your paper. Draw the pattern to fit the grid as shown on the pattern page.

Braiding
Lift the right hand strand and cross it over the center strand, so that it becomes the center strand. Lift the left hand stand and cross it over the center strand, so that it becomes the center strand. Continue crossing the right strand, then the left, to form a braid.

11 Arrange stuffing on the cardboard about 1 in. (2.5 cm) thick. Place the stuffing in a plastic bag. Arrange the stuffing in the bag and tape around the bag with masking tape to make it a similar shape to the cardboard.

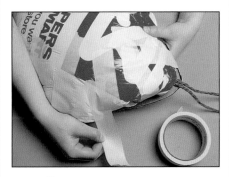

12 Lay the bag of stuffing onto the cardboard and tape it in place at the edges.

13 Lay the BACK piece right-side-up, on top of the bag of stuffing. Insert the tail and the hanging loop through the slashes in the fabric.

14 Turn the mouse over. Glue and tape the edges of the BACK fabric onto the cardboard at four points, top, bottom and the centers of each side.

If there isn't enough fabric, you have over-stuffed the bag. Cut a hole in the bag and remove some stuffing. Then try gluing the four points.

Now is the time to toss in some catnip, if you wish.

15 Glue and tape the edges of the back fabric to the cardboard between the four glued-down points. Snip into the edge of the fabric, wherever necessary, to help with shaping. Glue and tape well.

16 Apply glue near the edge of the cardboard side of the mouse. Lay the TUMMY piece onto the cardboard side, gluing the edges down. Allow to dry.

17 Here, Kitty, Kitty, Kitty!

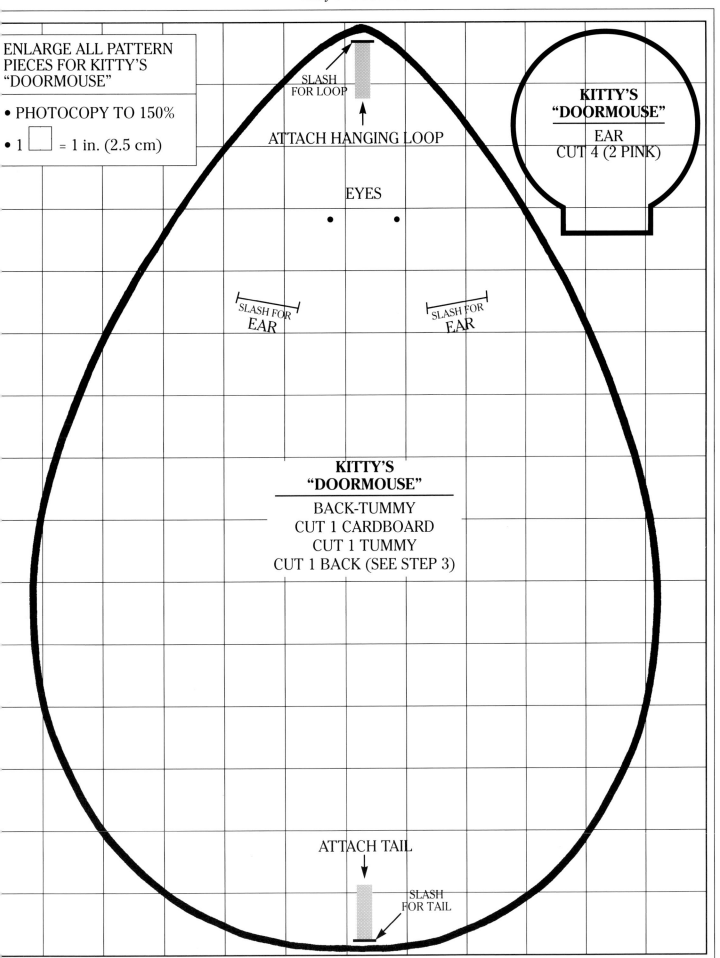

ENLARGE ALL PATTERN PIECES FOR KITTY'S "DOORMOUSE"

• PHOTOCOPY TO 150%

• 1 ☐ = 1 in. (2.5 cm)

SLASH FOR LOOP

ATTACH HANGING LOOP

EYES

SLASH FOR EAR

SLASH FOR EAR

KITTY'S "DOORMOUSE"

BACK-TUMMY
CUT 1 CARDBOARD
CUT 1 TUMMY
CUT 1 BACK (SEE STEP 3)

KITTY'S "DOORMOUSE"

EAR
CUT 4 (2 PINK)

ATTACH TAIL

SLASH FOR TAIL

Rolling "Stones"

The fabulous pieces of jewelry shown in these pictures are all made from rolled-up paper. The colors and designs of your paper can make the beads look like stone, marble, wood or bright plastic. No two are ever exactly the same, which makes them fascinating. Use wrapping paper or magazines for your beads. Part of the fun is finding the magazine pages in the colors that fit your idea. You'll be looking at magazines in a whole new way.

Rolling paper beads is a very old craft. We've updated it with easy, new jewelry ideas. Just add bits and pieces of unwanted costume jewelry and a few pennies worth of beads to make a brooch, a hair clip, a necklace, or earrings.

Here are the basic instructions for rolling paper beads and four different jewelry projects. When you purchase your seed beads, buy fairly large ones so you will be able to push your needle through.

How to do it

Paper Bead

What You Need

- wrapping paper or magazine pages
- scissors
- glue stick
- hair pin
- *Optional:* drinking straw

1 Cut a triangle from the paper, about 2 in. (5 cm) or less across the bottom and 10 in. (25 cm) tall.

Whatever *width* you cut the bottom of the triangle will be the *length* of the finished bead.

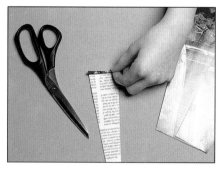

2 Lay the triangle wrong-side-up. On the bottom, (the shortest edge), fold up a very narrow piece. Fold it twice more.

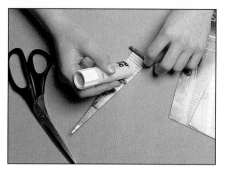

3 Begin rolling the folded edge. Starting is the trickiest part, so don't give up.

When you are half-way along the triangle, spread some glue onto the paper. Continue rolling over the glue.

Spread glue onto the point of the triangle, making sure it is completely covered. Roll to the end. Clamp the end in place with a hair pin. Allow the glue to dry.

4 To make a chunky paper bead with a large hole, follow step 1. Then, cut a length of a drinking straw to match the bottom of the triangle.

Glue the bottom of the triangle to the straw. Finish by rolling up the paper with the straw inside. Follow step 3 to finish.

Brooch

What You Need

- materials for paper beads (see "Paper Bead", this page)
- flat 3-hole clasp
- large seed beads
- thread to match your beads
- beading or darning needle, at least 2¼ in. (6 cm) long
- craft glue

1 Make eight to ten paper beads in a variety of lengths. (See "Paper Bead", this page.)

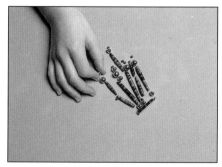

2 Lay the clasp on a table top with the pin down and the closure at the right-hand side. Lay the paper and seed beads in place the way you want them, ending each row with a seed bead.

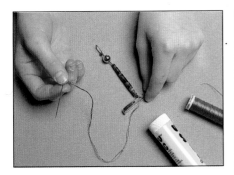

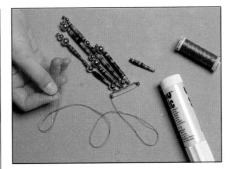

3 Using the needle, threaded double, tie the ends of the thread in a knot through the left-hand hole of the clasp. (See *Loose Ends* in the "Read Me" section.)

String a row of beads, ending with one seed bead. Skip over the end seed bead and go back through all of the beads. Bring the thread back through the hole on the clasp.

4 Slip the needle and thread through the center hole on the clasp twice. String another row.

Do this again so that you have two rows hanging from the center hole.

5 Repeat step 4, but this time use the hole at the right-hand side of the clasp.

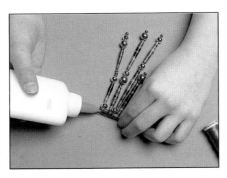

6 Using the craft glue, stick a paper bead onto the top of the clasp. This will hide the threads.

Give your jewelry as a gift in a beautiful Jewelry Box. (See page 94.)

Read Me

Make It Easier
To prevent beads from rolling around, try working on a piece of velvet or velour.

Rolling Paper
If the rolled paper springs open or if you want to tighten the bead, hold the edges of the rolled paper between your thumb and first finger. Gently pull the flat paper with the other hand.

Everyone has their own style of rolling the paper. Some pick the triangle up and roll with their right hand, using the left hand to keep it from unrolling. Others prefer rolling the bead on a flat table top. Experience will help you find out which way you like best.

Loose Ends
When you tie your first knot, use your glue stick to stick the loose ends to the thread. When you start stringing beads, be careful that the first few beads hide the glued-down ends.

Adding Thread
To add more thread while you are stringing the beads, don't wait until you run out. Instead, cut the thread while there is some left. Thread the needle again, tie the ends of the old thread to the ends of the new thread and stick the loose ends to the thread.

Tying Off
When tying off the thread, be careful to have the right tightness. If it is too tight, the beads won't hang nicely. If it is too loose, you will see gaps between the beads.

To hide the last knot, tie it before a long bead. Apply glue to the thread near the knot. Then draw the thread through the long bead and cut the thread.

Hair Clip

What You Need
- materials for paper beads (see "Paper Bead", page 50)
- a spring-type metal hair clip
- pleated ribbon or bow
- craft glue
- large seed beads
- darning or beading needle, at least 2¼ in. (6 cm) long
- thread to match your beads

1 Lay the hair clip with the clasp down and the closure to the left. Spread craft glue onto the hair clip. Stick pleated ribbon or bow on clip and sew in place.

2 Make eight to ten paper beads in varying sizes. (See "Paper Bead", page 50.)

With the hair clip as described in step 1, arrange the beads, ending each row with a seed bead.

3 Using the needle and thread, stitch through the center of a pleat or the bow.

String a row of beads. Go back through the row of beads, but skip over the seed bead at the end of the row.

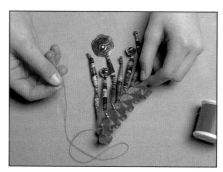

4 Stitch through the ribbon or bow to start a new row.

Repeat step 3.

Continue stringing rows of beads until you are finished. Then tie off on the wrong side of the hair clip.

Necklace

What You Need
- materials for paper beads (see step 5 under "Paper Bead", page 50)
- large beads with large holes
- long thin shoelace (a man's shoelace for dress shoes is good)

1 Roll eleven to fifteen chunky paper beads. (See step 4 under "Paper Bead", page 50.) You will need an odd number for the necklace to balance.

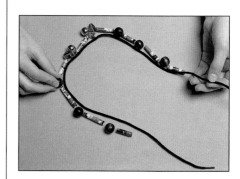

2 Arrange all of the beads in a row beside a shoelace to figure out how you like them.

3 String the beads onto the shoelace. When they are all strung, hold the necklace in place on your neck to test how it hangs. If it doesn't hang well, restring your beads in a more balanced arrangement.

4 Tie the ends of the shoelace together. Make sure it will fit over your head.

Earrings

What You Need

- materials for paper beads (see "Paper Bead", page 50)
- large seed beads
- 2 earring hooks
- darning or beading needle, at least 2¼ in. (6 cm) long
- thread to match your beads

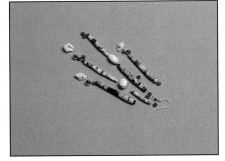

1 Make ten to twelve paper beads in different lengths. (See "Paper Bead", page 50.)

Arrange one earring hook and the beads the way you want them, ending each row in a seed bead.

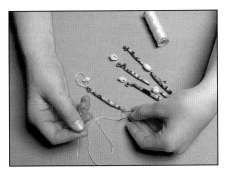

2 Thread the needle and tie the ends of the thread through the ring of the earring hook. (See *Loose Ends* in the "Read Me" section.)

String a row of beads onto the thread, ending with a seed bead. Go back through all of the beads, skipping the end seed bead.

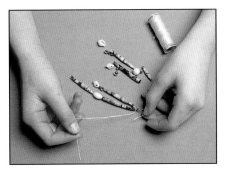

3 Draw the needle and thread through the ring in the earring hook. String the next row of beads in the same way.

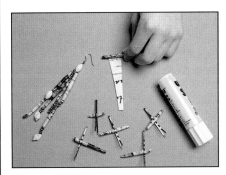

4 Continue until all the rows have been strung. Tie off your thread. (See *Tying Off* in the "Read Me" section.)

Make the second earring in the same way, rolling more beads if necessary. Make the second earring as different from the first as you like.

Decorator Basket

These baskets look as though they were bought in an expensive craft shop, yet they cost very little to make. All you need is some rope and scrap fabric and you can make them while watching TV.

Use any type of rope that is handy. If you buy your rope, the bright yellow nylon type is the cheapest and the easiest to find. The finished size of the basket depends on the thickness of the rope you use. Thin rope will make a smaller basket than thick rope.

When you make your basket, choose the color of the fabric to suit the person or their place. You can also give a favorite, worn-out shirt or scarf new life as a basket! Prints make a more interesting basket than plain colors, although using several plain colors can create a cheerful, striped effect.

Beginner's time for making a basket: one to two hours.

How to do it

What You Need

Materials
- ½ yd. (.5 m) fabric
- masking tape
- 6 yd. (6 m) medium weight rope
- craft glue

Tools
- scissors
- ruler
- measuring tape
- pen

Optional For Handle
- 2 ft. (60 cm) nylon rope
- light-weight wire
- ⅛ yd. (.2 m) fabric
- needle and thread

Finished Size

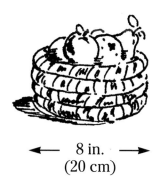

← 8 in. →
(20 cm)

1 Tear five to ten strips of fabric about 1½ in. (4 cm) wide. (See *Tearing Fabric* in the "Read Me" section.) If your fabric won't tear, cut strips with scissors.
    Set the fabric strips aside.

2 Wrap masking tape around the ends of the rope to prevent fraying. Measure and mark, but don't cut the rope.

3 Lay the end of one fabric strip onto the rope so that it hangs over the end by about 3 in. (8 cm). The strip should be on an angle, as shown. Tape it in place.

4 Begin wrapping the fabric strip around the rope. Keep the strip angled, so that it overlaps onto itself. Try to keep the wrapping tight.

5 When you come to the end of the first strip, tuck a second strip under the end. The two strips should overlap by about 4 in. (10 cm). Continue wrapping as tightly as possible.

6 Continue wrapping and adding strips, until the rope is covered to your mark. Tape the end of the strip to the rope, but don't cut the rope.

7 Go back to the beginning of the rope. Tuck and fold the overhanging end of the strip around the end of the rope, gluing it in place. Stitch if necessary.

Tear eight narrow strips about 24 in. (60 cm) long and ¾ in. (2 cm) wide. Put four of the strips aside.

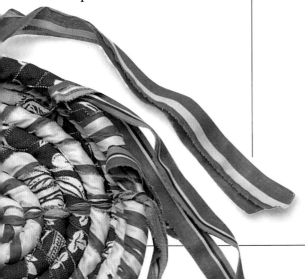

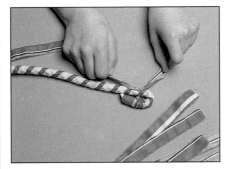

8 Tie the center of one narrow strip to the finished end of the rope, in a single knot.

Bend the covered end of the rope over, using the narrow fabric strip to tie it to the adjoining rope.

Tie the remaining three narrow strips to the rope, with equal spaces in between.

Read Me

Tearing Fabric
Try to choose a fabric that tears. Woven cotton fabrics are best. Sometimes wovens will fray when torn. Cut or pull away loose threads.

Knits such as sweater and T-shirt knits won't tear. You can cut these knits with scissors, but it will take much longer.

Pinning
If your basket-coil unwinds, you may want to pin it together, especially for the first few coils, until you get the hang of it.

Coiling
As you wind the coil, it helps to lay it on a hard, flat table top. Keep it even and smooth looking.

Shaping
If you want the sides of your basket to be V-shaped, rather than straight up and down, don't place the coils directly on top of each other. Instead, put them slightly off-center toward the outer edge.

Optional Handle

9 Begin to coil the rope. Whenever you come to a strip, tie it around the rope. The first couple of coils are the trickiest. The strips get in the way and the coil looks like a crazy sea creature. It goes faster and easier, if you can find someone to help hold it. Don't give up. It gets easier. (See *Pinning* and *Coiling* in the "Read Me" section.)

11 To make the sides of the basket, continue to coil the rope. But place the rope on *top* of the last coil, not beside it. (See *Shaping* in the "Read Me" section.) As you pass over the strips, tie them over the rope. Continue until you reach the mark on your rope, where the wrapping ends.

13 Bend a piece of rope and hold it in position on the basket, like a handle. Cut it to the length you want. Wrap the ends of the rope with masking tape.

Using light-weight wire, wind it around the rope, leaving an extra piece, 1 ft. (30 cm) long, at each end.

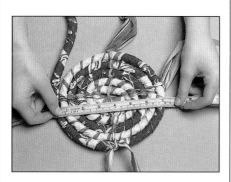

10 Continue to coil the basket until the coil is 7 in. (18 cm) across.

Using the four extra strips, tuck them between the last two coils. Space them evenly apart between the ties. Pull the strips through halfway and tie each in a single knot.

12 If you are happy with the size of your basket, cut the rope and finish the end as you did for the other end, gluing the strip in place. (See the first part of step 7.) If you want the basket to be bigger, cover more of the rope and continue coiling the basket.

Trim the loose ends of the ties 1 in. (2.5 cm) from the knot. Then glue and tuck them between coils. Or you can tie the loose ends of the ties into decorative bows.

14 Bend the handle, placing the ends of the rope on each side of the basket at the ties.

Loop the excess wire around the top coil securely several times. Bring it back up to wrap around the handle. Tape down the ends of the wire.

15 Tear several fabric strips 1½ in. (4 cm) wide. Wrap a strip around the top coil of the basket, covering any wire. Then wrap the handle, gluing as you go. Be sure no rope or wire is showing. Stitch where necessary.

A plain cardboard box is easy to dress up with theme pictures, funny tabloid headlines or comics. Tie it all up with a crepe paper bow.

Baby, Baby, Baby!

Baby is funny and cuddly, with her button nose and silly little smile. Using a real baby sleeper makes her a realistic size. Get the smallest sleeper with feet that you can find, one made for a newborn. A used, or discount sleeper is fine for Baby.

Baby's head, hands and body are all made from panty hose. The body, which is inside the sleeper and won't be seen, can be made from a used pair, while the head and hands should be made from a new pair. For the new panty hose, try to get a large or queen-size pair that has a sheer toe, not a reinforced toe. Remember the color becomes much lighter when the panty hose is stretched. It's a good idea to file your nails before you start to work on Baby. Otherwise there might be some snags on Baby's face.

Beginner's time to make Baby: three hours.

How to do it

What You Need

Materials
- a new pair of panty hose for head and hands
- 1 lb. (500 g) white polyester stuffing
- medium rubber band
- heavy thread to match panty hose
- 2 buttons, googly eyes, T-shirt paint, 2 craft eyes, or needle and thread for eyes
- piece of fake fur 3 in. (8 cm) square
- small baby sleeper (newborn size)
- thread to match collar and cuffs of sleeper
- used pair of panty hose, for body

Tools
- scissors
- ruler
- darning needle
- pins

Optional
- craft glue
- blusher and make-up brush

Finished Size

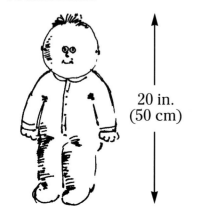

20 in. (50 cm)

1 To make the arms, measure from one toe of the new panty hose and cut a piece 7 in. (18 cm) long. Do this again with the other toe end. The toe ends will become the baby's hands.

2 Fill the arms half-way with stuffing. Tie thread next to the stuffing. These are the elbows. (See *Rubber Bands* in the "Read Me" section.) The stuffed half should be plump and round.

Fill the tops of the arms with stuffing. Tie the ends shut. (See *Tying* in the "Read Me" section.)

3 Tie a wrist on each arm about 1½ in. (4 cm) from the toe ends. (See *Rubber Bands* in the "Read Me" section.)

To make fingers, use a darning needle and thread and sew four very big stitches on one hand, pulling each stitch tight. Do this again with the other hand. Set the arms aside.

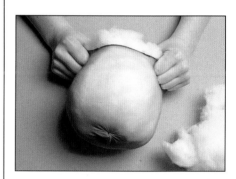

4 Make the head. Measure and cut a length of new panty hose 7 in. (18 cm) long. Tie one end shut. (See *Tying* in the "Read Me" section.) Turn the head inside-out so that the knot is inside. This is the top of the head.

Form a ball of stuffing as big as a melon. Push the stuffing into the panty hose and tie the open end shut. It should be firm. This knot will be the neck. The head should be about 5 to 5½ in. (12 to 14 cm) across.

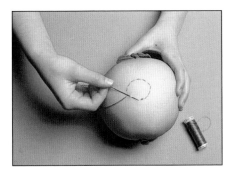

5 Start making the face. Use a darning needle, threaded double with heavy thread and knotted, for all sewing steps that create the face.

To make the nose, sew a circle about 1½ in. (4 cm) across, just below the center of the head. Use medium-sized stitches. Pull the stitches tight to gather, checking that there is stuffing in the nose.

Tie off, but don't cut the thread.

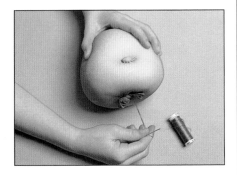

6 Make the cheeks. Push the needle through the top of the nose and out through the knot at the neck. Pull it very tight. Tie off and cut the thread.

You may think the face looks pretty strange, but don't give up. It improves with every step.

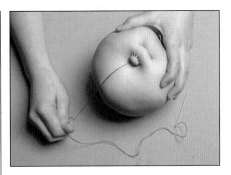

7 Make the mouth. Push the needle into the top of the nose, coming out halfway between the nose and the bottom knot. Make a huge stitch, about 1½ in. (4 cm) across. Bring needle back out at the top of the nose. Pull it very tight. Tie off and cut the thread.

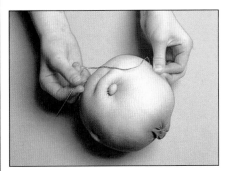

8 Make ears by grabbing and stitching a pinch of panty hose on each side of the head. They should be about level with the nose.

Read Me

Tying
When tying a panty hose end shut, pick up two "corners" and make a square knot. Don't tie a knot in a length, because this uses up too much panty hose.

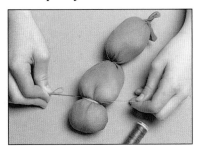

Rubber Bands
To make tying thread around the panty hose easier, wind a rubber band around the panty hose. Tie thread (doubled) tightly, next to the rubber band. Remove the rubber band.

Eyes
If the doll is for a baby, be certain the eyes you choose can be attached securely. Babies under three years of age tend to pull eyes off and eat them.

Boy or Girl?
If you wish to make it clear that your doll is a boy or a girl, tie or stitch a pink or blue bow into its hair. Or use yellow, red, orange or purple for either.

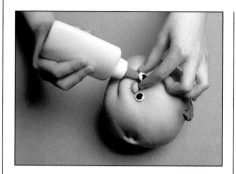

9 Make eyes by sewing dots, by painting dots, or by gluing on craft or googly eyes. If you want a sleepy baby, make two stitches in black or brown thread for closed eyes. (See *Eyes* in the "Read Me" section.)

10 Cover Baby's knot and give her hair by gluing or stitching a piece of fake fur over the knot.

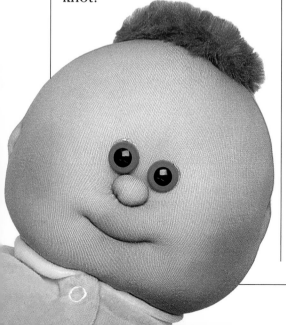

11 With the sleeper closed, pin the head in place. Using thread that matches the neck of the sleeper, sew on the head. Set the fat-headed, droopy baby body aside.

12 Start making the body. For this you will need the top of the used panty hose with its legs attached.

Measure down from the crotch 10 in. (25 cm) on both legs and cut the panty hose.

Tie thread around each leg at the crotch.

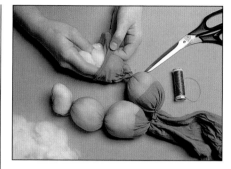

13 Fill each leg half-full with stuffing. Tie thread around each leg at the end of the stuffing. These are the knees.

Fill each leg two-thirds with stuffing. Tie thread around each leg again. These are the ankles.

Fill the ends of the legs with stuffing. Tie them securely shut. These are the feet.

14 Stuff the top of the panty hose so that it is plump and squishy. This will be the baby's chest.

Roll the waistband of the panty hose over and sew it down. It will form "tabs" at the ends for attaching the arms. Baby's body is certainly strange looking, but remember, it won't be seen.

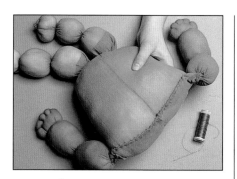

15 Sew the knots at the ends of the arms to the "tabs" on the body.

17 *Optional:* To give your baby rosy cheeks and lips, use a makeup brush to brush on some blusher.

18 Give Baby a hug.

16 Open the sleeper and put the body inside. The hands should stick out of the sleeves and the feet should be in the feet of the sleeper.

Sew the head to the top of the body.

Make a strong stitch through the bottoms of the feet and into the panty hose, so that the feet won't pull out.

Sew any openings in the sleeper shut, so that Baby won't get undressed.

Paper bags with handles can be made to suit the gift or the person to whom you are giving the gift. Cover logos or other markings with theme pictures – Barbie, Elvis, tabloid headlines, baby, cat, horse, dog or pig pictures.

Doggie Deli

All dogs have favorite words – *walk*, *out*, *car* and most of all *cookie!* Fang will love his very own easy-to-make biscuits. These homemade treats are tasty and good for him, and they'll help clean his teeth. We tested them on the dogs we know and they gave our biscuits ten wags, a paws-up and begged for more.

Most small dogs can't manage a big cookie. If the biscuits are for a small dog, cut them into small squares, triangles or round cookies with a knife, and remove them from the oven after the first twenty minutes of baking.

For larger dogs, make the croissant, eggbread and bagel shapes, as shown in the instructions. The doggie's owner will love the way they look as much as Fang loves the taste! Just be sure to wrap them up in the Doggie Bag (page 85) so your friend won't eat them instead of giving them to her pooch.

Beginner's time to make biscuits: twenty minutes preparation, one hour, twenty minutes baking.

How to do it

What You Need

Ingredients
- 1¼ cup (325 mL) all-purpose flour
- package of orange cheesy powder from macaroni-dinner-in-a-box
- 2 tbsp. (30 mL) chopped parsley (it's good for Fang)
- ¼ cup (50 mL) water
- an egg
- milk

Tools
- measuring cup
- mixing bowl
- glass
- fork
- mixing spoon
- cutting board
- knife
- cookie sheet

Optional
- sesame seeds and poppy seeds
- butter or margarine
- cookie cutters

Yield
Makes 8 large dog cookies or 20 small ones

1 Preheat your oven to 350°F (175°C).
Put the flour, the cheesy powder and the chopped parsley into a mixing bowl. Stir with a fork.

2 Measure the water into the measuring cup and set it aside.
Break the egg into the glass and mix it with the fork.

3 Pour the egg into the water. Stir the egg and water mixture.

4 Pour the egg and water mixture into the bowl with the dry ingredients and mix them with the mixing spoon. It will be difficult to blend all of the ingredients together, but they will eventually blend and become dough. You may need to pick the dough up in your hands and knead it.

5 The dough should be stiff. Sprinkle flour onto the cutting board. Lay the dough on the cutting board. Sprinkle more flour on top. Roll, press or stretch the dough until it is about ¼ in. (.5 cm) thick.

6 For small-dog cookies cut the dough into small squares, circles or triangles about 1 in. (2.5 cm) across.

For large-dog cookies, either cut out dog bones with a cookie cutter or make bread shapes as follows.

Croissant
   Cut a tall triangle, about 3 in. (8 cm) across at the bottom. Roll it up. Bend it in a curve.

7 Place the biscuits on a cookie sheet. (If you don't have a non-stick pan, grease it with butter or margarine.) Brush some milk onto each biscuit. This will make them brown nicely. Sprinkle sesame or poppy seeds, as desired.

Bagel
   What's a deli without a bagel? Cut a circle about 2 in. (5 cm) across. Make a hole in the center. Plump it up by squeezing the sides.

Egg Bread
   Form a cylinder of dough. Fold it in half lengthwise. Twist the "legs" together. Join the ends.

8 Bake at 350°F (175°C) for twenty minutes. Set the timer. Cookies for small dogs should be removed when the timer sounds. Let sit to cool and harden.

   Continue baking cookies for large dogs, turning the oven down to 200°F (95°C) for another sixty minutes. (Put the timer on again so you don't forget them.) Allow to cool and harden.

Photo Frame

Make this gorgeous photo frame from things that might otherwise be thrown away – paper or fabric scraps. It's a great way to recycle! By choosing carefully, you can make a frame to suit anyone. If someone you know has recently decorated, you might be able to use some of their matching material or wall paper.

This project takes some patience, but the result makes it very worthwhile. An adult may need to help you cut the cardboard with an art knife.

If you are covering your frame with paper, wrapping paper works best. You can also use pictures from last year's calendar or even a magazine. Use a glue stick for sticking the paper.

Fabric is trickier to work with than paper. If you use fabric, try to get craft glue that is very sticky. Sometimes it's called "super-tacky". You can also use white carpenter's glue.

Beginner's time for Photo Frame: two to three hours.

How to do it

What You Need

Materials
- paper and pencil
- medium-weight cardboard
- corrugated cardboard
- fabric or paper, for front
- plain paper to match front
- 6 in. (15 cm) ribbon
- masking tape

Tools
- push pin
- ruler (metal-edged is best)
- art knife
- scissors

Finished Size

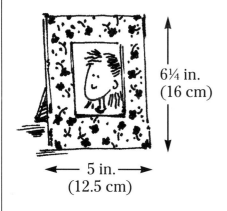

6¼ in. (16 cm)

5 in. (12.5 cm)

1 Using a pencil and ruler, trace the pattern pieces on pages 74 to 77 onto paper. Then transfer the pattern pieces onto the materials stated on the pattern pieces. (See *Marking* in the "Read Me" section.)

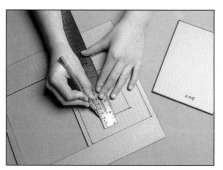

2 Using the art knife and ruler (or scissors for fabric), cut carefully along the lines. Score the easel, as marked on the pattern. (See *Cutting* and *Scoring* in the "Read Me" section.)

3 Lay the FRONT-PAPER (or FABRIC) piece wrong-side-up.
  Spread glue onto one side of the FRONT-CARDBOARD. Stick the cardboard onto the center of the wrong side of the paper (or fabric).

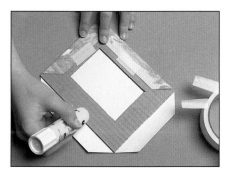

4 Apply glue near one edge of the cardboard. Fold the paper (or fabric) over, onto the glue. Hold in place with tape, if necessary. Repeat for the three remaining sides.

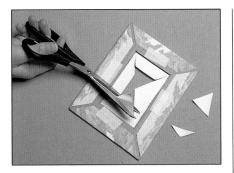

5 Cut an X in the center of the paper (or fabric) to the cardboard corners. Trim the points of the triangles.

Repeat step 4 with the inside edges.

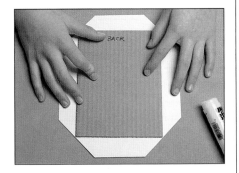

6 Repeat step 3, laying the BACK-PAPER piece flat and gluing the BACK-CARDBOARD piece onto it. Don't glue the sides yet.

7 Glue the INSERT-CARDBOARD piece to the BACK-CARDBOARD piece, matching the edges.

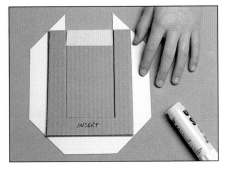

8 Cut from the edge of the paper to the inside edges of the insert, as marked on the BACK-PAPER pattern. Spread glue onto this flap of paper and fold it onto the cardboard.

Repeat step 4.

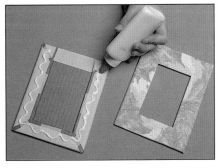

9 Lay the assembled back of the frame wrong-side-up.

Apply strong craft glue to the insert.

Lay the wrong side of the assembled front onto the glue, matching the sides. *Note:* If the design on your front has a top and a bottom, be sure that the top is at the open end of the insert.

Read Me

Make It Easy
Cut several small pieces of masking tape for later use.

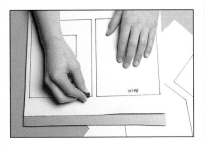

Marking
Lay the traced paper patterns on top of the cardboard or paper. Using a push-pin or another sharp object poke holes into all the corners. Use the pencil to mark the pin pricks, if necessary. Remove the paper and join the dots with ruler and pencil.

Cutting
When cutting with an art knife, it is better to make several light cuts along one line. Pressing too hard can make you lose control. Save your table by cutting on top of another piece of cardboard or a plastic cutting mat.

Scoring
To score a piece of cardboard, cut it lightly, about half way through, so that it is still together, but will bend where it has been scored.

10 Repeat step 3, gluing the EASEL-PAPER piece to the unscored side of the EASEL-CARDBOARD piece.

Repeat step 4. Score the paper along the score on the cardboard so that the easel can bend.

11 Glue the EASEL – FINISHING piece to the back of the easel, below the score line.

12 Apply glue to the back side of the easel, above the score line.

Position the easel in the center of the back of the frame, with the top edges matching. (Remember, the open end of the insert is at the top.)

Glue one end of the ribbon to the back of the frame, where it is shown on the pattern. Glue the other end to the easel, where it is shown on the pattern.

13 Using the pattern piece marked PHOTO, cut your photo (and a piece of clear plastic, if you wish) to the correct size. Place the plastic on top of the photo and slide them into the frame from the top.

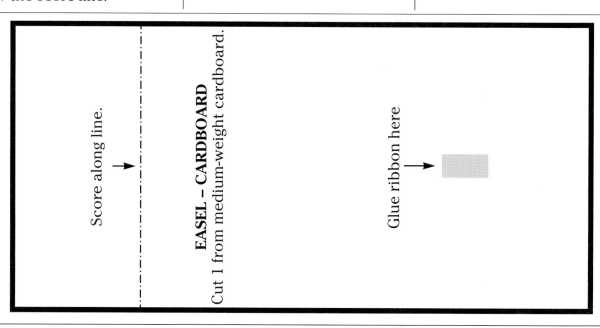

Score along line. →

EASEL – CARDBOARD
Cut 1 from medium-weight cardboard.

Glue ribbon here →

WAIT! DON'T CUT THESE PAGES.

If you cut out these patterns, you will destroy important information on the back of these pages. Instead of cutting, trace the pattern onto a sheet of paper.

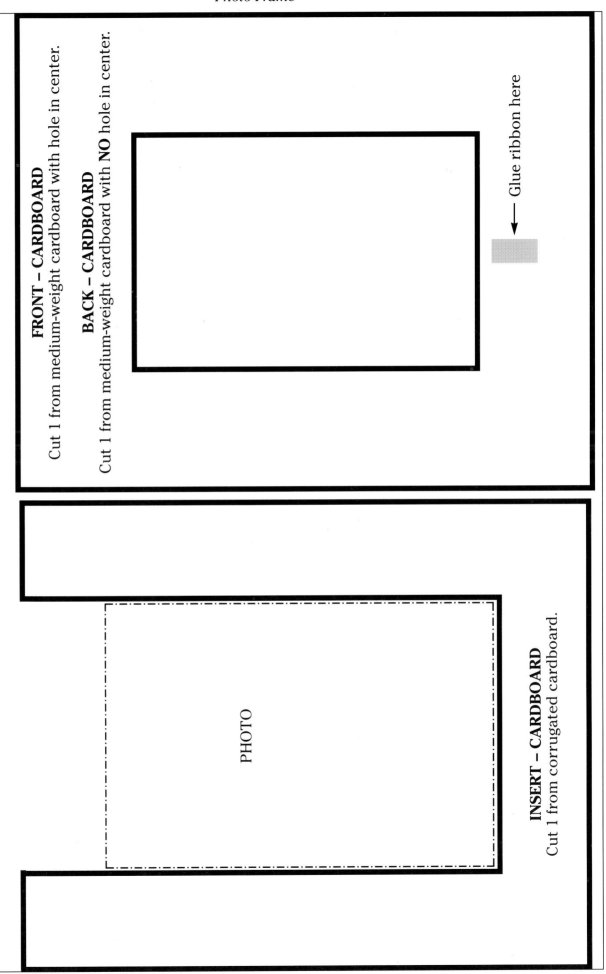

FRONT – CARDBOARD
Cut 1 from medium-weight cardboard with hole in center.

BACK – CARDBOARD
Cut 1 from medium-weight cardboard with **NO** hole in center.

Glue ribbon here

PHOTO

INSERT – CARDBOARD
Cut 1 from corrugated cardboard.

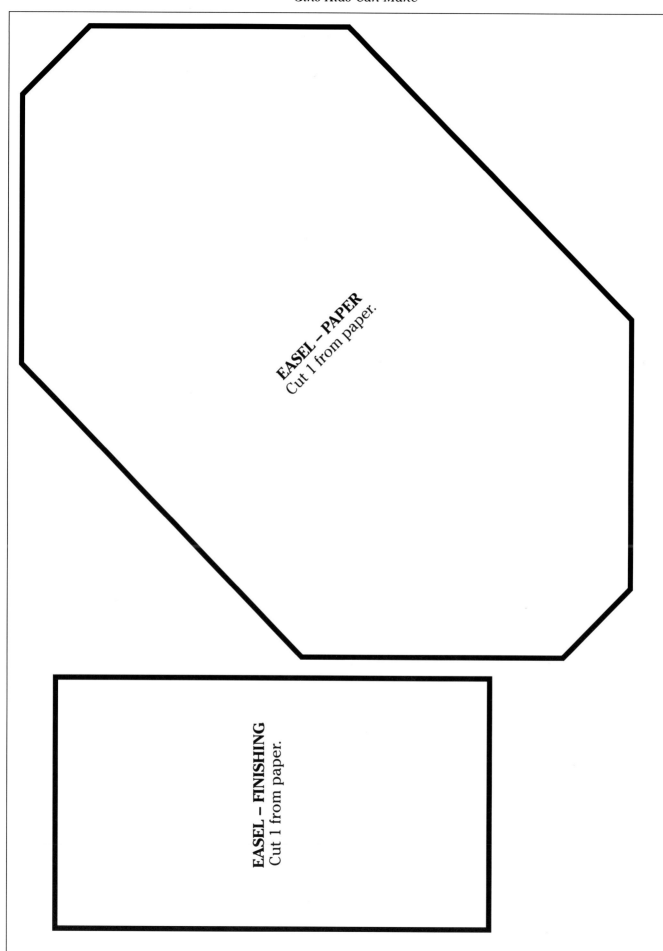

EASEL – PAPER
Cut 1 from paper.

EASEL – FINISHING
Cut 1 from paper.

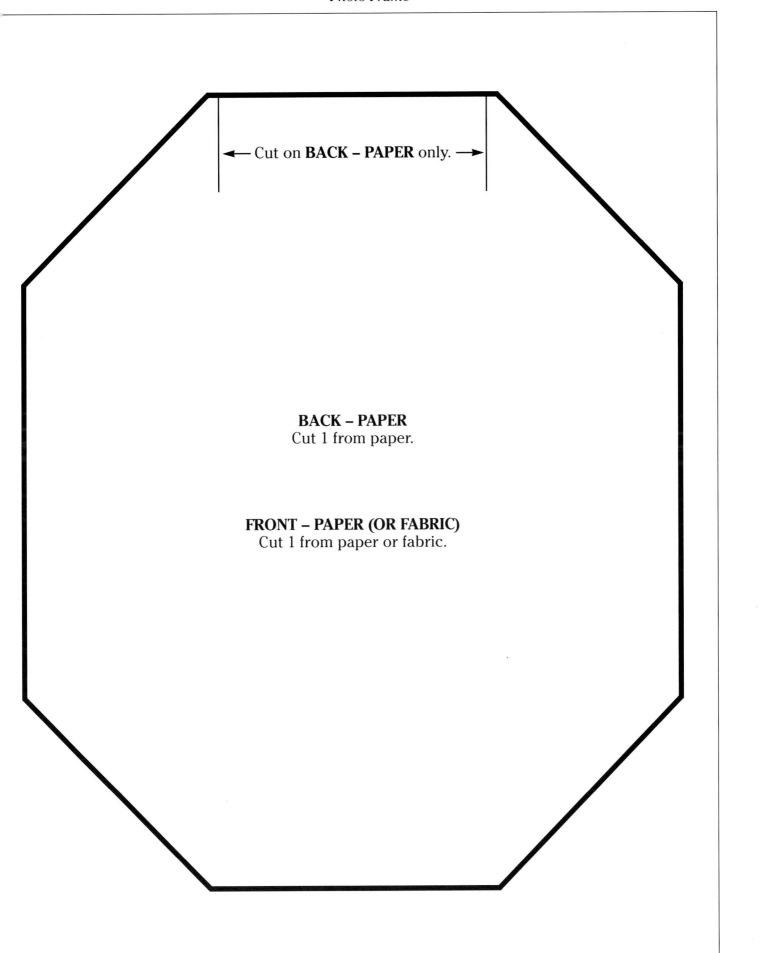

Cut on **BACK – PAPER** only.

BACK – PAPER
Cut 1 from paper.

FRONT – PAPER (OR FABRIC)
Cut 1 from paper or fabric.

Hobby Horse

If you have a toddler on your gift list, this is an ideal present. It's great for either a boy or girl. It's big and impressive, but costs very little to make. A hobby horse is one of those old fashioned, no-batteries-required toys that makes for hours and hours of happy play.

While this horsey isn't hard to make, it does take some time and you may need help cutting the broomstick. When you purchase the broomstick, the hardware clerk may cut it for you, if you ask, so take your measurements along.

You will need a new, man's-size work sock for the horse's head. You'll also need another sock or a knee-hi (a clean, used one is okay) for inside the horse. Once all of your materials are together, this horse is loads of fun to make, so giddy-up!

Beginner's time to make Hobby Horse: two to three hours.

How to do it

What You Need

Materials
- broomstick or 1 in. (2.5 cm) thick dowel, 34 in. (85 cm) long
- clean used sock or knee-hi
- 1 lb. (250 g) white polyester stuffing
- masking tape
- carpenter's glue or craft glue
- new work sock
- ball of chunky yarn, for mane
- 2 craft eyes, buttons or felt, for eyes
- thread to match ears
- square of felt for ear-backs
- square of pink felt for ear-fronts

Tools
- pencil or pen
- small handsaw
- scissors
- crochet hook
- pins
- sewing needle

Optional
- paint for broomstick
- 1½ yd. (1.5 m) of wide elastic or banding for bridle
- thread to match bridle

Finished Size

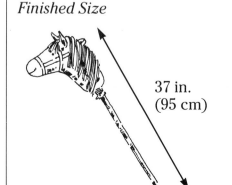

37 in. (95 cm)

1 *Optional:* Paint or stain the dowel or broomstick. Use any kind of paint that is waterproof when dry. Allow to dry.

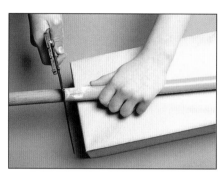

2 Measure 34 in. (85 cm) from the end of the broomstick or dowel and mark it. If using a broomstick, measure from the rounded end.

Get help from an adult to cut it, using a small hand saw. Remember: measure twice, cut once!

3 Using the knee-hi or used sock, place a handful of stuffing into the toe. Place the stuffed knee-hi over the cut end of the dowel.

4 Cut a length of yarn or masking tape. Dab glue onto the dowel under the knee-hi. Gather the knee-hi around the dowel. Tie the yarn (or wrap the masking tape) around the glued area. Set aside and allow the glue to dry.

5 Using the new sock, fill the toe tightly with stuffing.

6 Begin making the mane. Cut about 60 pieces of yarn, each 20 in. (50 cm) long. An easy way to do this is to make a long loop of the yarn many times. Then cut at each end.

7 Draw a line along the center of the sock, from the front of the heel to the ribbing. This marks the center line of the horse's mane.

8 At the heel end of the line, insert the crochet hook through the sock, under the line. Place the centers of three strands of yarn into the hook. Draw the strands through, making a loop.

9 Slip the six cut ends through the loop. Then pull the ends tightly. Repeat steps 8 and 9 close to the first loop. Continue along the full line, cutting more strands if needed.

Read Me

Eyes
If you are using craft eyes, (the kind used on teddy bears), push the post through the knitting of the sock without breaking the yarn. Make sure the washer is pushed tightly onto the post.

If you are sewing buttons for eyes, sew through a scrap of strong fabric on the wrong side for strength. When the buttons are sewn in place, apply glue under the buttons for extra strength.

If you have googly eyes, glue them in place. You can also glue or sew felt cut-outs. Or you can stitch yarn in place for eyes.

When your Hobby Horse is finished, you'll need to gift wrap it. We disguised ours as a big lollipop, in a variation of the Shaped Bag wrap. (See page 85.)

10 Attach your eyes, about 2½ in.(6 cm) from the point of the heel. (See *Eyes* in the "Read Me" section.)

11 Push the knee-hi end of the dowel into the head, fitting it into the heel. Fill the head very tightly with stuffing, all around the dowel.

Cut and put aside a length of yarn about as long as your arm.

Fold back the ribbing of the sock. Apply glue to the folded-up ribbing. This is easiest if you stand the horse on its nose.

12 Fold the ribbing down, so that the glue is in contact with the dowel. Wind the yarn tightly around the ribbing, keeping the mane free. Tie the yarn tightly. Allow the glue to dry.

Set the head aside.

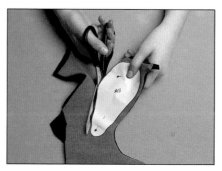

13 Trace the EARS pattern piece on page 83 onto paper. Pin the pattern to a double thickness of pink felt for ear-fronts. Cut along the cutting line. Repeat for the ear-backs.

Pin one ear-front and one ear-back together. Sew around the edge by hand or by machine. Repeat for the second ear.

14 Fold one ear in half, along its length. Position the wide end of the ear onto the side of the horse's head at the point of the heel. Pin in place. Stitch around the bottom of the ear. Repeat for the second ear.

Optional Bridle

15 From the elastic or banding, measure and cut 18 in. (45 cm) for reins.

Position the reins onto the horse's head with each cut end behind the toe of the sock, or the "nose". Pin in place. Stitch securely close to each cut end and on each side of the head in front of the ears.

16 Measure and cut 13 in. (32 cm) of banding. Position one end on the underside of the head, behind the nose. Stitch the end securely.

Apply glue on the side of the banding in contact with the head. Place the banding around the nose, covering the cut ends of the reins and overlapping the stitched end. It should be a snug fit, giving the horse's head some shape. Stitch the free end securely in place.

17 Measure and cut 14 in. (35 cm) of banding. Repeat step 15, but place this piece in front of the ears. Be careful not to catch the mane under the band.

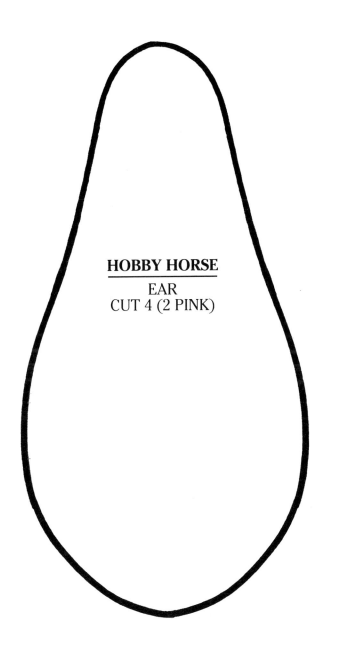

HOBBY HORSE
EAR
CUT 4 (2 PINK)

WAIT! DON'T CUT THIS PAGE!

If you cut out these patterns, you will destroy important information on the back of this page. Instead of cutting, trace the pattern onto a sheet of paper.

Wrap It Up

Bags

Shaped Bag

The following instructions are for a doggie bag, but you can make this bag any shape… heart, pig, tulip and so on.

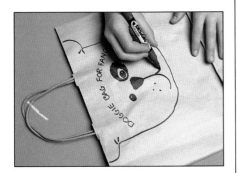

1 Using a paper shopping bag that has handles, flatten the bag and draw the dog's head on the bag so that the handles come out of its head.

Cut out the head, cutting through two layers of the bag.

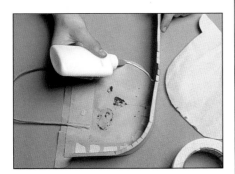

2 Cut a long piece of paper, 2 in. (5 cm) wide. Fold both long edges over ¼ in. (.5 cm). Using craft glue, stick one folded edge to the inside of the front of the bag, snipping into the folded edge to make it bend at curves and corners. Tape in place.

Repeat, gluing the other folded edge to the outside of the back piece of the bag.

Reusable Drawstring Bag

1 Cut two pieces of fabric 12 in. (30 cm) square. A knit fabric is a good choice for this, since it won't fray.

Place the squares with the right sides together. Pin well. Sew down one side, across the bottom and up the other side, leaving a 2 in. (5 cm) gap at the top of each side.

2 To make a channel around the top, fold the top edges down 1¼ in. (3 cm) onto the wrong side, tucking in the seam allowance at the side seams. Pin well. Stitch close to the edge.

3 Cut two lengths of ribbon or braid 38 in. (95 cm) long.

Turn the bag right side out. Thread a length of ribbon or braid through one hole in the side seam, through the full channel. Tie the ends together. (Attach a safety pin to the end of the ribbon to help guide it through the channel.)

4 Starting at the opposite side seam, thread a second ribbon or braid through the full channel. Tie the ends. To close the bag, pull the knotted ends of the ribbons.

Bows

Loopy Bow

1 Wind 1½ yds. (1.5 m) of ribbon, at least ¾ in. (2 cm) wide, into a loop 5 in. (13 cm) long. Pin the loop in the center.

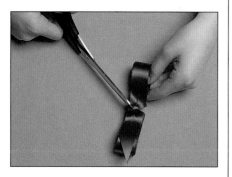

2 Cut a V into both sides of the ribbon, in the center of the loop.

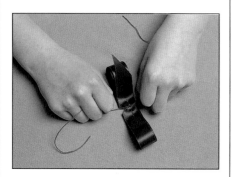

3 Using a piece of narrow ribbon or strong thread, tie a tight knot at the narrow point of the V's. Remove the pin.

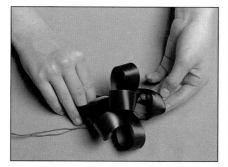

4 Separate and twist the loops. Use the ends of the center tie to attach the bow to your gift.

Plastic Bag Bow

1 Pile three or four colorful plastic bags on top of each other, matching one bottom corner. Measuring from the corner, cut a 12 in. (30 cm) square through all of the bags.

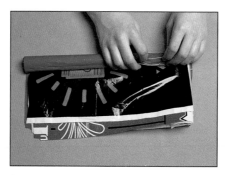

2 Starting at one side, roll the bags into a tight tube.

3 Tightly wind a rubber band around the bottom end. Cut into the opposite end, cutting to the rubber band, but not through it.

4 Cut again, close to the first cut. Continue cutting strips ½ in. (1 cm) wide until all of the tube is cut. You may wish to move the rubber band further up and cut off the rolled end.

Tie a bow made from a strip of the plastic bag or crepe paper to hide the rubber band.

Big Wraps

Flower Bow

1 Cut six pieces of tissue paper about 7 x 30 in. (18 x 75 cm). Lay them on top of each other. Make accordian folds 1 in. (2.5 cm) wide.

2 Tie a ribbon around the center of the accordian. Trim the ends of the accordian to be rounded. Spread the ends like a fan and gently begin pulling the tissue paper up towards the center, layer by layer, until all of the layers are fluffy and the bow looks like a flower.

The trees, paw prints and pigs were made by block printing on paper. The "cracker" is comic wrap. Recycling newspaper, foil or other "junk" is great for large gifts which can use a great deal of wrapping paper.

Comic Wrap

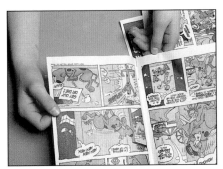

1 Use the weekend comics, tabloids or comic books. Remove the center staples if necessary, and separate the pages.

Apply glue along one edge of a flat comic page. Lay the edge of another flat sheet onto the glue.

2 Continue, adding more sheets until the comic wrapping paper is as large as you require. Allow the glue to dry and wrap your gift.

Crazy Christmas

Block Printing

1 To make a design on a big piece of paper, first cut a large raw baking potato in half lengthwise. Scratch a simple shape such as a fish, balloon, rocket ship, mouse or house onto the potato's cut surface. Use a pencil or pen for this.

2 Using a sharp, small knife, cut down around the shape and remove potato from around the shape.

Using a paint brush, apply paint to the raised shape on the potato and print it onto plain paper. Continue printing as many images as you wish. Allow the paint to dry. If you are printing on dark paper, print first with white. When the white is dry, print another color on top. You may wish to add details with markers or crayons.

Instead of throwing away that favorite T-shirt or sweatshirt that you've grown out of, give it years of new life as a large, crazy, Christmas stocking that will hold loads of loot!

1 Cut the neckband from the T-shirt, being careful not to cut into it. Set the neckband aside.

2 Draw a stocking shape onto your T-shirt. Try to get the favorite part of the T-shirt design into your stocking shape. If you want fringe or other parts of the T-shirt attached, mark these too. If you need help with the stocking shape, use a work sock, or another Christmas stocking as a general guide. changing the shape as you wish.

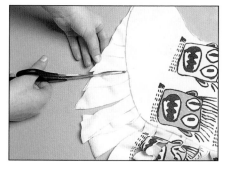

3 Cut along your outline, keeping fringe attached.

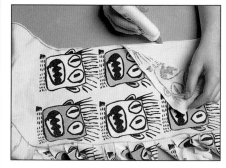

4 Squeeze a line of craft glue near the edge, on the wrong side of one stocking piece. Do not glue along the top. Place the second stocking piece on top, matching the edges. Allow to dry.

5 Using a needle and thread, hand sew a seam around the stocking, leaving the top open. This will make the stocking stronger.

Stocking

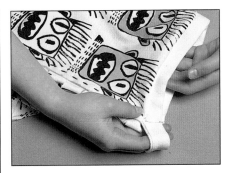

6 Find the neckband and pin it to the top of the stocking, with the cut edges together. It will be too big. Let the extra piece form a loop at the back of the stocking, for hanging.

7 Sew the neckband to the stocking, close to the cut edges. Turn the neckband up and top stitch the loop at the back seam.

8 If you wish, decorate your stocking with T-shirt paint, sequins, lace or other interesting stuff you can find around the house.

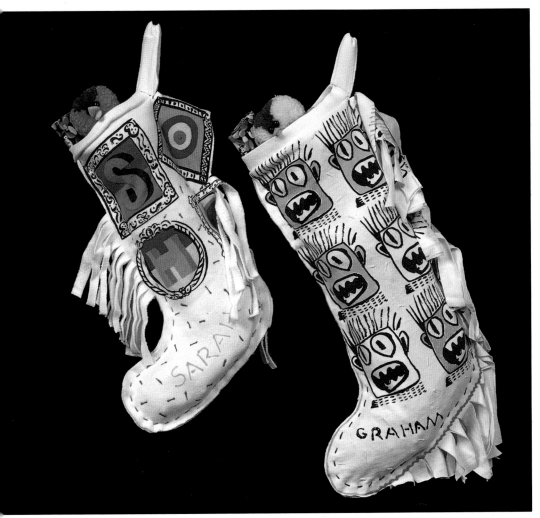

Two old favorite T-shirts become two new favorite stockings. The size of the shirt decides the size of the stocking.

Envelope Wrap

Pyramid Box

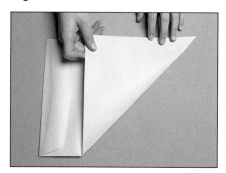

1 Fold the bottom corner of a large envelope over to the opposite side.

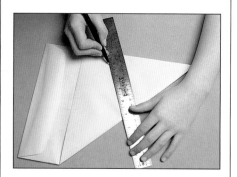

2 Measure 7 in. (18 cm) along each side from the point. Draw a line across the envelope to make a triangle shape.

3 Measure 3 in. (8 cm) up from the center of the first line. Draw a triangle on top of the first line. Cut along this triangle.
  Make holes in the tops of the triangles.

4 Open the pyramid, reversing the center fold.
  Fold the points to the center. Place the gift inside. Thread ribbon through the holes and tie.

Ice Cream Cone

1 Follow steps 1 and 2 of the Pyramid Box, but this time measure 4 in. (10 cm) along the sides. The triangle will be the "cone".

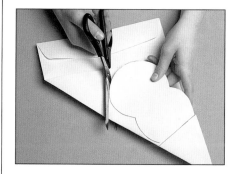

2 Draw two bumps, like circles, above the line. These will be the "ice cream". Cut around the bumps.
  Color the ice cream and the cone.

3 Open up the cone, reversing the center fold. Make holes at the tops of the ice creams. Place the gift inside. Thread ribbon through the holes and tie.

Valentine

1 Follow steps 1 and 2 of the Pyramid Box.
Using a compass, place the point in the center of the line and draw a half circle from side to side, on top of the line. Cut along the half circle.

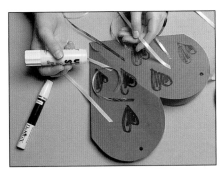

2 Open up the heart and decorate it as you wish. Make holes at the top-center of the Valentine. Place the gift inside. Thread and tie ribbon through the holes.

Envelope gift packages are perfect for small gifts such as jewelry, candy or a pair of socks or gloves. From left: Ice Cream Cone, Pyramid Box, Valentine.

Cards

High-Tech Cards

1 Cut one piece of light-weight cardboard and 1 piece of corrugated wrapping board (or cardboard), both 3½ x 9 in. (9 x 23 cm).

Cut 1 piece of craft paper 7 x 9 in. (17 x 23 cm).

2 Decorate the bumpy side of the corrugated wrapping board. Make holes to tie on decorations, such as comics, stamps, lace, photos, or bits of jewelry and beads with ribbon or by sewing. (Things cannot be glued to corrugated board.)

3 Lay the corrugated wrapping with the decorations down. Lay the cardboard piece next to it, matching the sides. Glue the craft paper onto both pieces. Allow to dry. Fold shut.

Embossing and Burnishing

1 Cut one piece of heavy paper 7 x 9 in. (18 x 23 cm). Fold it in half lengthwise. Set it aside.

Find a flat object, such as money, chain, earrings or a medallion, which will give you an interesting design.

2 Lay the objects in a pleasing pattern on a small dry, soft sponge. Wet a piece of light-weight or bond paper. Lay it on top of the objects.

Place another dry, soft sponge and then a phone book on top. Allow the paper to dry. It will take at least one full day.

3 Lift the phone book and the top sponge from the objects, but don't remove the paper. Keeping the paper on the objects, scribble with a pencil or crayon to accent the shapes of the hard objects. Remove the paper from the objects.

From left, two High-Tech cards, two Ruffled cards, two Embossed and Burnished cards and one Ruffled card.

Ruffled Cards

4 The paper will have an interesting texture from the sponge. Trim the edges near the embossed image.

Cut and glue a colorful or patterned piece of paper to the front of the heavy paper (the fold is at the top or left side).

Apply glue to the edges of the wrong side of the embossed image and stick it to the front of your card.

1 Cut a piece of heavy paper, or light cardboard 7 x 9 in. (17 x 23 cm). Fold it in half lengthwise. Set it aside.

Cut an interesting picture or design from a magazine or an old calendar (or make one yourself) 3 x 8½ in. (7.5 x 22 cm).

2 Cut a slash in the picture where you would like the ruffle to start.

Cut some tissue or crepe paper. Crunch one end and insert it in the slash, gluing it to the wrong side.

Apply glue to the wrong side of the paper with the ruffle. Stick it to the front of the folded paper. The fold should be to the top or left side. Decorate if you wish.

Boxes

Jewelry Box

1 To make the top, measure and cut an 8 in. (20 cm) square of paper. Picture pages of an out-of-date calendar are great for this.

On the wrong side, measure and mark an X at the center.

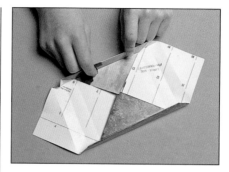

2 On the wrong side, fold two opposite corners to the center.

Measure, mark and fold the two folded edges over ¾ in. (2 cm).

3 Open out the folded corners. Repeat step 2 with the remaining two corners.

4 Bring the two open corners back to the center, folding the excess paper into neat triangles that tuck underneath the sides. Glue down the points.

Make the bottom of the box the same way, but this time cut the paper 7¾ in. (19.5 cm) square.

Soft Box

1 Cut one piece of corrugated wrapping board or light cardboard such as bristol board, 4 x 12 in. (10 x 30 cm). If using corrugated wrap, the ridges should run *across* the cut piece.

Cut a second piece the same length, but ½ in. (1 cm) narrower.

2 Cut both ends of both pieces into points.

Take one piece and bend it, so that the ends overlap. Staple it in place. Repeat with the other piece.

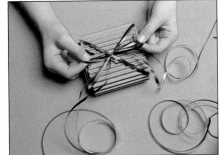

3 Place the gift into the narrower box section. Slide it into the other box section.

4 Tie with ribbon.

The boxes in this section are small and best suited to jewelry and other little gifts. Try making them from different papers for variety.

ABOUT THE AUTHOR

Sheila McGraw is the author of *Soft Toys to Sew* (Firefly 1992), *Papier-Mâché for Kids* (Firefly 1991) winner of the Benjamin Franklin Award, *Papier-Mâché Today* (Firefly 1990), co-author and illustrator of *My Mother's Hands* and *My Father's Hands* (Medlicott Press, Simon and Schuster 1990-1991), author and illustrator of *This Old New House* (Annick Press 1989), and illustrator of the bestselling children's book *Love You Forever* (Firefly 1986).

Sheila lives in downtown Toronto. She works from her house that is home to a multitude of papier-mâché beasts, soft toy monsters, works-in-progress and her marmalade cat Clawdia (as seen on page 42). She is the mother of two sons.

ACKNOWLEDGEMENTS

Thank you to everyone who worked with me on this book: Lionel Koffler for making the book possible, Pamela Anthony for her assistance, ideas and her perseverance, Joy von Tiedemann for her brilliant photography, Elizabeth McGraw for her hands in all the how-to pictures, my editor Sarah Swartz for her super-fast editing and her input, all the kids who modeled for photos and the parents who brought them. Thank you to all of the people who work behind the scenes producing and printing this book and to the people at Firefly Books who look after countless details.